THE WORLD IN COLOR PHOTOGRAPHY

480 PHOTOGRAPHS IN FULL COLOR

© Illustrations: Colour Library International Ltd. 1977
© Text: William MacQuitty. 1977
© Foreword: Arthur C. Clarke. 1977
First published in Great Britain in 1974
Second edition published in 1977

Produced by Ted Smart C.L.I.

Filmsetting by Focus Photoset Limited, 90-94 Clerkenwell Road, London EC1M 5TE

Printed in Italy by Poligrafici Calderara - Bologna

ISBN 0-517-217031

This edition published by
Crescent Books,
a division of Crown Publishers, Inc.

Inquiries should be sent to:
Colour Library International (U.S.A.) Ltd.,
163, East 64th Street, New York, N.Y. 10021.
Tel. 212 737-7171 Telex 125068

CRESCENT BOOKS   NEW YORK

Contents

Foreword

It may seem strange that someone who has spent much of his life discussing ways of escaping from the earth should now introduce a book devoted to its beauties. However, poachers make the best game-keepers, and it is no coincidence that we became generally aware of our environmental problems at the very moment when we obtained the first views of Earth from space. As astronaut William Anders said when he returned after circling the Moon in Apollo 8: "We looked back from 240,000 miles to see a very small, round, beautiful, fragile-looking little ball floating in an immense black void of space. It was the only colour in the universe—very fragile—very delicate indeed. Since this was Christmas time, it reminded me of a Christmas Tree ornament—colourful and fragile. Something that we needed to learn to handle with care."

We are beginning to learn that lesson, perhaps just in time. Though much has been destroyed, this book shows how much of our planet's beauty, strangeness and wonder still remains. The writing of the text, by my friend Bill MacQuitty has been a labour of love—a tribute to the world he has enjoyed in a busy life of exploring and film-making. I am sure that all his readers will share that enjoyment—and will be equally determined to cherish and preserve the planet which, however far they wander, men will always call Home.

Arthur C. Clarke
Colombo, Ceylon.

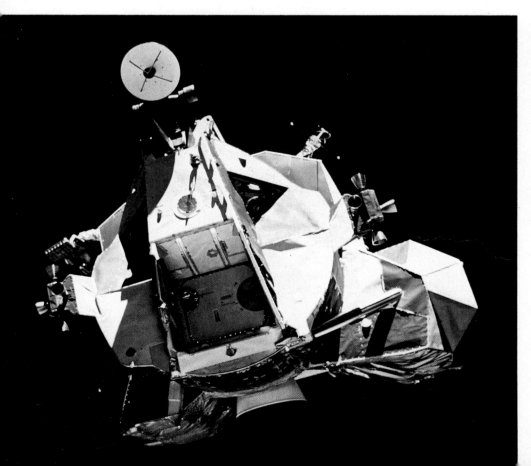

Introduction

The best of all possible worlds may well be the one on which we live. Certainly it looks very good to those who see it from outer space, its rich blues and greens swathed in swirling streamers of white cloud. What a teeming complex of life, what a variety of scenes it contains, but we tend to take its wonderful contents as a matter of course and occupy ourselves with business affairs. We look through spectacles that are seldom clear and bright but often flawed or out of focus, making the world drab or sad to our subjective eyes.

This book gives the reader a new look at over fifty countries which are grouped in six sections for easy exploration—Europe, Africa, North America, South America, Eurasia and the Pacific. A disciple of an Indian Guru said how pleasant it would be if the whole world were covered with skins so that the thorns and sharp stones that beset their path would be rendered smooth. The Guru replied how much simpler to wear sandals. Modern man wears wings and travels with an ease, security and comfort beyond the wildest dreams of even the wealthiest of the early voyagers. Alexander the Great, Marco Polo, Dr. Livingstone and Sir Richard Burton never enjoyed the luxury that even the most economy minded tourist commands today, but they had one advantage that perhaps we are in danger of losing. They were intensely interested in their journeys and in all the new sights and customs they discovered. Their attitude towards the world was full of zest and curiosity. How can our modern generation recapture this urge for living, this appreciation of our earth?

All known life on earth depends upon two things, energy supplied by the sun, and water. Had the earth been closer to the sun its water would have evaporated into gas; had it been further away the water would have been frozen solid. Fortunately for us the sun is at just the right distance to allow water to exist as a liquid and it was in this liquid that life originated. When living organisms ventured out of the water on to the land they brought the water with them in the first space suits—their skins. Just as our spacemen are able to live on the moon by bringing their environment with them so the world's first land creatures brought the essentials of life; we still have the sea in our blood.

Then there is the extraordinary circumstance of our personal survival. We are all links in chains of life that reach back a hundred thousand generations to the beginning of man on this planet; one hundred thousand occasions when our ancestors provided children to continue the chain of life unbroken to the present time. This makes us very special guests at the banquet of life, and provided man in his stupidity does not destroy our world there should eventually be an abundance for all.

Meanwhile how best to enjoy this feast? Undoubtedly we should be foolish to take our own environment with us when we go to look at the world. We should polish our spectacles and focus them with objective clarity on the strange new customs and scenes that greet us. The ideal traveller should forget from whence he came and whither he is going. His interest should lie in the immediate scene which he should assimilate with relish. It is not easy to be an ideal traveller for we have grown up with the loves, hates, greeds, envies, angers and fears belonging to our long past. Our struggle for survival is largely over but our instincts and prejudices remain and stand in the way of our enjoyment. The sabre-toothed tiger is extinct, but our hair still rises in the presence of danger. In our shrinking world man now accepts that foreigners and foreign lands, though strange, have much to offer.

The following pages provide a sample of the world and its beginnings, an indication of what is available and where. For armchair travellers it provides the cream of many journeys and the essence of many places. Through these pages one can journey imaginatively, reach one's destination and see the sights; perhaps with a feeling of awe and excitement as our spaceship earth journeys on its incredible voyage.

Left. Bryce Canyon Utah U.S.A.

EUROPE and the Near East

Over the past million years much of Europe has been submerged beneath the Atlantic Ocean. Vast ice caps advanced and retreated from the North Pole flooding the dry land as they melted and withdrawing huge quantities of water when they froze. Europe still bears the scars of the ice ages, particularly noticeable in the deep fjords of Norway which were gouged out of solid rock by the tremendous pressure of the glaciers. Between the northern ice sheets and the Mediterranean stretched a bleak wilderness, the great plain of Europe across which wandered small groups of Neanderthal men. For 150,000 years these sub-men managed to survive these daunting conditions, sheltering in their fire-warmed caves during the coldest periods, but some fifty thousand years ago they vanished completely, possibly exterminated by the early Palaeolithic or stone age people who had gradually come into the area as the climate became warmer.

The newcomers had one outstanding skill, they could draw and paint better than any of the other inhabitants of the earth. Splendid examples of their art are to be found in the famous caves of Lascaux in France and Altimira in Spain. The walls of these caverns burst into life with pictures of men and animals exuberantly painted in pigments of white, black, yellow, brown and red still looking as fresh as the day they were done thirty thousand years ago. As well as painting they sculpted small figures out of soapstone or ivory, often fat females, doubtless part of fertility cults. Gradually later stone age people and other tribes followed the first arrivals and in 5,000 B.C. the age of bronze began.

The finest culture to rise from this mixture of races was born in Athens about six centuries B.C. Here was founded the first democratic state. This was not democracy as we know it, for only citizens who lived inside the city could vote and it was withheld from slaves or even freedmen. A century later Athens joined other Greek city states to form a league of defence against Persia. The magnificent ruins of Persepolis, Shiraz, and numerous other sites record this influence that was to affect the future of art. Her sculpture as well as her architecture had a simplicity and beauty of proportion which still remains an example to the world. The Parthenon built of white marble on the massive rock of the Acropolis is an outstanding achievement of this ability. Greece also led the world in drama, literature, law, schools, universities, stadiums, the Olympic games and much else. Rome too had similar success. From a collection of small villages on the river Tiber she gained vast dominions on which she imposed peace, law and order, roads and communications. The west owes much to Rome's enduring influence which is reflected in our constitutions. During the thousand years of her rule Rome assembled the greatest empire the world had so far seen, but her better claim to immortality was her ability to nourish the cultural achievements of the Greek world that she had conquered and to spread them across Europe. Roman architecture, art and literature bear the stamp of Roman power and assurance but show the influence of Greece. This impressive civilisation continued until Constantine founded Constantinople in 325 and Christian Byzantine civilisation replaced pagan Greek culture in the eastern Mediterranean. The occasion was marked by the building of the great church of Santa Sophia, dedicated on Christmas Day 538. When the Turks captured the city in 1435 the church was turned into a Mosque, the Hagia Sophia, and Constantinople became Istanbul, but its history was not to end there. In 1935 on the order of Kemal Ataturk it was made into a museum but the visitor standing beneath the huge dome cannot fail to sense its original use. Close by in Lebanon another change took place. Baalbek, the vast temple devoted to the worship of Baal, was altered to Heliopolis after the Egyptian city of the sun-god Amun. Later under Alexander the Great it became the Temple of Jupiter. All that remains are six of the original fifty-four pillars. Near by stand the descendants of the famous Cedars of Lebanon which Solomon used to build a palace for himself and a temple for the Ark of the Covenant, the divine symbol of the ancient Hebrews.

In the winter of 406 the Rhine froze and this most unusual event may have accelerated the course of history. Some fifteen thousand barbarians with their families crossed the river into the Roman province of Gaul. They met with little resistance and slowly travelled southwards looting and plundering. In 410 Rome was sacked and the final collapse of Classical civilisation made way for the Early Middle Ages. Waves of warlike tribes kept Europe in a constant state of turmoil, but at the same time infused it with some of their abundant energy. As in Ancient Egypt wild animals were made deities for their strength and fertility, but in the long run they were no match for organised Christianity which had survived the fall of Rome and risen above the chaos. In 481 Clovis, King of the Franks married Clothilde, a Catholic princess of Burgundy and was himself baptised a Christian. The faith spread rapidly and was brought as far as Ireland by Saint Patrick. The Irish monks proved extremely zealous and soon sent missionaries back to England and the Continent, where they expounded their own interpretation of the Gospel. The Irish church was a beacon of light in the darkness of the Early Middle Ages.

In 768 Charlemagne inherited the Frankish throne and the power of the church was further strengthened when Pope Leo III unexpectedly crowned him Emperor on Christmas Day. In spite of its growing strength Christianity failed to capture the imagination of the Moslem States which after the death of Mohammed in 632 energetically extended their territory from the confines of Arabia to an area bounded in the east by the river Indus and stretching to Spain and the Atlantic Ocean. The expansion led to internal strife and after seven Crusades by the West the might of Islam began to weaken but not before it had made a deep impression on the life and architecture of Europe.

Gradually the dark days of Europe began to be illuminated by a rebirth of interest in individuals rather than causes. About 1300 the Renaissance introduced a new approach to art. In place of the designs of Islam and the formality of Byzantine art there was a swing towards reality. Human anatomy was reproduced in the smallest detail. Flowers, jewels, buildings and furniture were shown for the first time, with accurate perspective and the old aesthetic concepts gave way to scientific considerations. It was almost as if photography had come into being. This great surge of individual art produced artists like Leonardo da Vinci and sprinkled Europe with shrines and monuments, cathedrals and castles filled with perhaps the most beautiful sculptures, paintings and objets d'art known to man.

At the beginning of the sixteenth century the countries of Europe began to look outwards to explore the world. The Spanish, Portuguese and Dutch, like the Vikings of old, sent their ships sailing away to found colonies in distant lands. Power seemed to move from east to west and it was left to Britain, the most westerly part of Europe, to found the greatest empire of them all. These tribal islands repeatedly invaded by savage Norsemen united in 1066 under their last invader, William of Normandy. The British were a curious, stubborn, valiant and inventive people. They were adept in administration and improvisation. Their inventiveness sparked off the Industrial Revolution. Steam was harnessed to drive their mills and ships. Small scale business with small employers became large scale production under big employers. Markets were required for the increased production and soon merchant adventurers like the East India and Hudson Bay companies were competing with similar companies in Europe for foreign markets. Sir Walter Raleigh's expedition to America had already led to the founding of Virginia in 1606. In 1759 Wolfe took Quebec and Canada was ceded to the British by the French in 1763. From these excursions the British Empire emerged, a mixture of growths and accumulations like no Empire before it, but guaranteeing peace and security and for this reason sustained and endured by the subject races. The British gained much wealth from their Empire, but they gave it law and order, roads and hospitals, schools and universities, and above all the democratic ideal. The British Empire is no more, but Britain is still a power-house of ideas, having given the world radar, penicillin, hovercraft as well as leading sculptors, artists and writers—her heritage from the civilisation of countries of Europe of which she is now a member.

Modern Europe covers 3,900,000 square miles, measuring 2,400 miles north to south and 3,000 from east to west with a population of 533,000,000. To journey through this fascinating land whose stormy history is recorded in ancient buildings and monuments, in precious works of art in paint and sculpture, in delicate and flamboyant jewellery, in music, food and wine is to savour the essence of many civilisations. Here are more treasures than the rest of the world can show, here for the moment is the cultural culmination of man's long journey through the ages.

BRITAIN

On these and the following six pages are shown a selection of the pageantry, the abundance of unique and historic buildings, the people and the unforgettable landscape that go to make up the British Isles and that act as a magnet, attracting visitors from all over the world.

SCANDINAVIA

Scandinavia, covering Norway, Denmark and Sweden is symbolised by the midnight sun *below*. Fishing is a major industry in the Lofoten Isles and from centres like Bergen, shown *bottom right* on market day.

The nomadic Lapps *far right* range across the whole of northernmost Scandinavia. Of Asian origin they live by herding reindeer which they follow as it migrates across the frozen north.

19

Copenhagen is the most cosmopolitan of Scandinavian capitals, catering for avant-garde as well as traditional tastes. Tivoli Gardens *above* is a pleasure park and has the oldest mime theatre in Europe and *top right* Hans Christian Andersen's Little Mermaid looks out to sea.

Norway's coastline is deeply cut by fjords *left* which, with its glaciers and waterfalls, form a major tourist attraction.

Sweden is a land of lakes, rivers and forests such as at Tannforsen *right*. Its spacious and elegant capital Stockholm, too, is set on numerous islands.

HOLLAND

Gouda *below* has a
traditional cheese market.

Amsterdam *right* on the River Amstel is the major commercial city and an important centre of the diamond trade. It has over 400 bridges crossing its network of canals.

Great areas of Holland have been created by man. The reclaimed land is protected from submersion by the sea by the winding canals with their typical features of wooden bridges and windmills.
At Kinderdijk *below right* sixteen windmills still turn on windy days.

LUXEMBOURG

The Grand Duchy of Luxembourg is an independent state of only 999 square miles, south of Belgium.

Bruges, the city of bridges, *below* originated in the 7th century at a bridge over an inlet of the sea. The Belgian capital, Brussels, is a bustling modern European centre and has in the Grande Place *overleaf* one of the finest squares in Europe. Flower and pet markets take place surrounded by the 15th century Hotel de la Ville and the 17 famous Guild Houses.

BELGIUM

FRANCE

Place-de la Concorde *opposite top left* and Sacre Cœur *opposite top right*.
Versailles *bottom right* was built for Louis XIV and in 1682 the whole court moved there. The gardens by Le Notre are amongst the most beautiful in the world and surround two smaller chateaux; the Grand Trianon and the Petit Trianon, favourite residence of Marie Antoinette.

At the juncture of 12 avenues known as L'Etoile in the centre of Paris stands the Arc de Triomphe *below* commissioned by Napoleon to depict his coronation and battles.
Paris *overleaf* can justly be described as the romantic capital of the world and it attracts artists, today, just as much as it always has.

Mont St. Michel *left* is a granite islet in the Bay of St. Malo. A Benedictine Abbey is perched on its 240 feet high peak.

Along the Loire and its tributaries lie many famous chateaux and vineyards. Chinon *left* is a castle set above the town. It was here that Joan of Arc told the Dauphin of her mission. Luynes *bottom left* was the home of the Duke of Luynes, Constable of France and soldier under Louis XIII. The renaissance chateau at Chenonceaux *top right* is constructed over the River Chen. In 1535 it was given by Henry II to Diane of Poitiers from whom it was taken by Catherine de Medici.

Chambord, east of Blois, *bottom right* stands in 13,000 acres of walled park and is the largest of all, with over 450 rooms. Molière gave the first performance of Le Bourgeois Gèntilhomme there in 1670.

PORTUGAL

Portugal has retained much of its traditional character and relies heavily on old crafts and agriculture. It is a strongly religious country and at Fatima the Statue of Christ *left* marks the site where the Virgin Mary is said to have appeared to three young girls in 1917. It is now a place of pilgrimage.

The Algarve with its moorish associations and Estoril *opposite top right* are popular tourist areas while the traditional industries of fishing and wine still flourish. At Sesimbra *middle right* fishermen land and sell their catch of Pes Espada swordfish.

Portugal's long history as an
adventurous seafaring nation is
commemorated by the monument
to Prince Henry the Navigator in
Lisbon *right*.

35

The two main religious influences of Spain have left impressive monuments. The still-strong Catholic church has created the inspiring cathedral in Barcelona *left* while the influx of the moslems in the early 14th century has given the south of Spain monuments such as the Alhambra at Granada. The Court of Lions *right* is named after the fountain at its centre. The Spanish countryside *overleaf* remains largely unchanged.

GERMANY

Whitwashed walls under a clear blue sky; the excitement of the Bullfight and the colour and music that are all so typical of Spain *left.*

Neuschwanstein *below* is the most complete, as well as the most fantastic, of Ludwig's creations with its scenes from Arthurian legends on the walls. Heidelberg *overleaf* on the river Necker has a splendid castle high on the river bank as well as the oldest of Germany's universities.

Vineyards *overleaf* as far as the eye can see slope down to towns and villages on the banks of the river.

The town of Berchtesgarten *left* acquired notoriety when it became Hitler's mountain retreat, far removed from the more traditional pleasures of a village band *below*.

The Rhine flows 850 miles through Holland, Switzerland and Germany and provides important communication links as well as the splendid vineyards dotted with ancient castles, such as Burg Katz *right* which produce some of the world's finest wines.

Cologne Cathedral *right* with its twin 515 feet high towers is one of the world's most striking gothic buildings. The foundation stone was laid in 1248 but work was still continuing into this century.

Nymphenburg Palace *left* a short ride from the centre of Munich was the baroque summer residence of the Kings of Bavaria in the 17th and 18th centuries. In its grounds are a porcelain factory which is still in operation, as well as the Amalienburg, a rococo pavilion by Cuvillès.

SWITZERLAND

Berne, *top* the capital of the Swiss confederation is one of the best built towns of Europe. Dating from the time of Charlemagne it has a magnificent cathedral, fountain and clock tower.

Zurich *above* is the banking centre of Europe and the most important business centre of Switzerland.
Geneva *left* lies on Lake Geneva, the largest stretch of water in Switzerland and is an important international centre. Mont Blanc looks down on the town which dates from the 16th century. The 458 feet high water spout has become its internationally recognised symbol.

The Town Hall, Vienna *below* is a
former Hapsburg palace part of it
dating from the 13th century.

The former Imperial Summer Residence of the Hapsburgs at Schonbrunn *left* has over 1000 rooms and was built in 1695. Like the Belvedere Palace and its famous gardens *right* also in Vienna, it is a magnificent piece of Baroque architecture.

The Austrian countryside is dotted with small towns and villages with their small churches as at Scheffau *right* often concealing magnificent interiors, and castles such as Festung near Salzburg *bottom right*.

ITALY

Overleaf may be seen some of the many famous landmarks that are to be found in Italy, followed by the quite unique city of Venice, now under threat from the very waters that gave it its quality and beauty.

Milan Cathedral *below* was built by the Visconti Dukes of Milan and is the second largest gothic cathedral in Europe. St. Peter's, Rome *right* took 120 years to complete and the combination of Michelangelo's design for the church and Berini's colonnades make it one of the most impressive squares in the world.

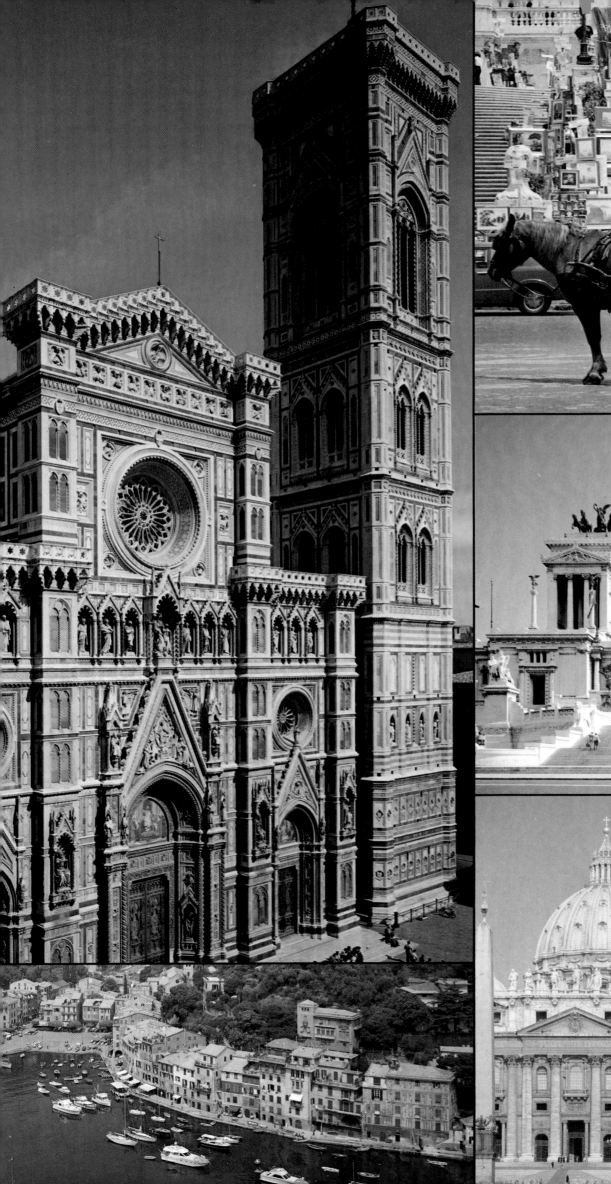

GREECE

Athens, the capital of Greece, is dominated by the Acropolis *right* the great flat topped rock on which was built the Parthenon and the other temples all dating from the 5th century B.C. Many of the original marble statues and facings now lie in other countries.

The names of the Greek islands have a magic which is all their own. Samos, Lesbos, Naxos and Crete have made an indelible impression on history. Largely untouched, but beginning to be discovered by tourists, the major islands such as Hydra *top* still rely heavily on the fishing industry. Similarly, Rhodes *above, left and far left* with its Byzantine windmills and fine mediaeval castle.

In Eastern Greece which includes that most ancient and tragic of cities, Thebes, lies Delphi the greatest spiritual centre of ancient Greece. Against the towering cliffs of Parnassus can be seen a complex of temples including the circular Temple of Athena *left* at which those wishing to consult the Oracle made their offerings.

A Greek orthodox monastery *below* is perched high on the cliffs at Meteora. Originally access was by net and pulley but now it can be reached by steps.

This group of islands in the mediterranean has important catholic and naval connections. St. Joseph holds the infant Jesus over the Church of St. Mary, Malta *left* while relics of an ancient belief are the Eyes of Osiris painted onto fishing boats at Xlendi, Gozo, *below* to ward off evil spirits. The Grand Harbour, Valetta, *bottom* is the scene of visits by the great naval powers.

overleaf
Dubrovnik, founded in the 7th century, at one time rivalled Venice as a trading port. Today with its fine 17th century cathedral and the 15th century clock tower it is an important holiday centre.

MALTA

YUGOSLAVIA

RUSSIA

Leningrad was founded by Peter the Great in 1703. It has many splendid reminders of the Romanovs. The golden domes of St. Saviour's chuch *middle right* give some idea of its richness.

Samarkand *below left* is the oldest city in the Republic of Uzbeckistan and it is here that Tamurlaine's memorial, and the tomb of his great love, lie.

A memorial to a modern hero, Lenin, is seen *below* at a stop on the Trans-Siberian Railway.

Yalta *bottom* scene of the meeting between Churchill, Roosevelt and Stalin is now the most popular Soviet holiday resort.

The Summer Palace *top* and *left* is perhaps the most splendid of the Romanov creations, with even the fountains being gold.

Moscow, on the River Moskva, has been the capital of the USSR since 1918. The general view *above* includes the modern buildings of the University which dwarf the secret city of the Kremlin with its gold-domed cathedrals *opposite bottom right*.

HUNGARY

The Danube flows through Budapest,
capital of Hungary *below* with the
remnants of the ancient castle on the
Buda bank and parliament House on
the Pest Bank.

The so-called Pillar of Absalom *below* is on the road to Kidron.

The splendour of the Dome of the Rock in Jerusalem *overleaf*.

Alongside the great advances of modern Israel
many of the people still rely on the land either
as shepherds *above* or on small farms or
collectives to produce the goods seen in the
covered markets *left* in Jerusalem.
The following two pages are devoted to views
of the people and places to be found in this
most remarkable and historic of cities.

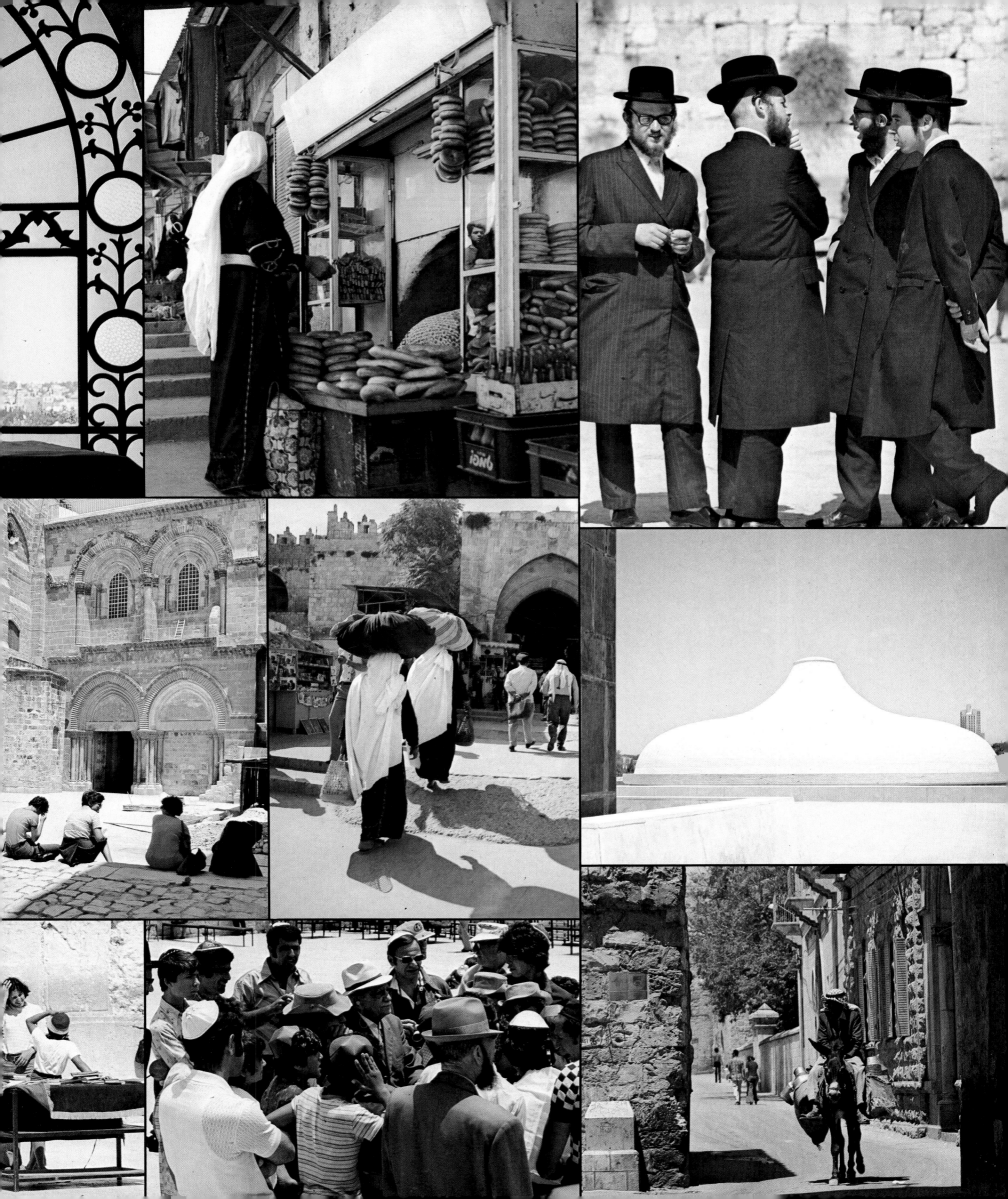

The growing importance of Iran
based on oil resources represents a
new wealth to surpass even the
breahtaking splendours which we
associate with Persia of old. The
magnificent Peacock Throne *left* is in
the Golestan Palace, Teheran, along
with a splendid collection of carpets
and tapestries.

The varied peoples of Iran are benefitting
from the revenues of the oil fields while
still retaining much of their ancient
heritage and simple ways. Islam is the
main religion and the teachers and
guardians of the Mosque like the one at
Shah Reza *above* are important members
of the community

A Bahktiyari tribeswoman and her
family are seen *right* in a caravanserai.

AFRICA

Africa is the second largest continent in the world, after Asia. Here it was that the earliest signs of man were discovered. The fossil remains of 'Homo Habilis' reputed to be 3,800,000 years old, were found by Richard Leakey in the Olduvai Gorge, in Northern Tanzania. These were tool-using men and probably the true ancestors of modern man. The great tribes of Africa still remain and continue to live in patterns of culture that have changed little since the dawn of history. Foreigners have come to Africa but it was only in the extreme south that Europeans were able to establish themselves and breed in this vast untamed land. Elsewhere the Africans were secure in the hold on their land, unlike the Indians of North America and the Aborigines of Australia who quickly succumbed to the floods of people from Europe and became dwindling minorities in their own countries.

This extraordinarily varied land covers over eleven million square miles with a coastline of sixteen thousand. The climate ranges from the eternal snows and ice of the highest mountain, Kilimanjaro, and the great Ruwenzori Range to the burning sands of the Sahara and Kalahari deserts. In the centre lie almost a million square miles of rain drenched equatorial forests, whilst bordering the deserts are the endless grasslands scattered with scrub and bush. Here and there through this sea of grass lonely beobab and acacia trees stand out offering shelter to leopard and vulture. Throughout this geographical abundance, all manner of men, beasts, birds, insects, fish and reptiles thrive, each adapted to its own area.

To the early explorers it was a dark mysterious continent filled with savage beasts and people. This simple notion was, of course, nowhere near the truth. The world owes much to the peoples of this vast land. In modern terms no computer could work today if it had to operate with Roman numerals. It was the Arab who supplied the system of numbers that is used by the civilised world. It was here in the valley of the Nile that the first delicate seeds of spiritual thought and scientific approach to life gradually took root and bloomed. Like the flooding Nile the surprising ideas of these remarkable people flowed out into the world around them. In this early period some six thousand years ago, three other civilisations were stirring, the Sumerian in the valley of the Tigris and Euphrates, that of the Indus Valley and the Chinese on the Yellow River, but none of these reached the level achieved by the people of the Nile Valley or affected Western Civilisation so much.

Forty-five centuries ago hieroglyphs on stone and papyrus recorded a way of life that still captures the fascinated attention of the world. Here were mysteries beyond the imagination of modern times. Rulers regarded as gods incarnate governed a number of African races who produced temples, monuments, statues and carvings, intricate tombs covered with delicate wall paintings and cut thousand ton obelisks in one piece from the rose-hued granite of Aswan with only primitive tools of stone and copper. With the same tools they produced delicate carvings on the hard surface equal to the finest work available today. Perhaps more astonishing was their ability to convey these huge obelisks to all parts of their country and erect them where they chose. The world appreciated these treasures so highly that they adorn the principal squares of many capital cities. One stands in the centre of the Place de la Concorde in Paris, others in Rome, London and New York. It is scarcely surprising that the last remaining wonder of the Ancient World should be theirs, the Great Pyramid of Gizeh, built by Cheops between 2650 and 2550 B.C.

The riches of Africa do not end with the valley of the Nile. In the south lie the greatest diamond mines and the richest gold fields in the world. More interesting than these treasures beneath the earth are the living treasures, the multitude of wild life that wanders across its surface. In the endless plain of Serengeti, the great crater of Ngorengoro and many other game sanctuaries the visitor can gaze on scenes of infinite beauty, vast herds of animals moving and living as they did before the advent of man, the balance of nature at work. The elephant and rhinoceros devouring the tough bush and pushing down trees to forage on the leaves and bark, thereby provide more light and space for the grasses. The giraffes delicately reaching for food in the upper branches whilst the herbivores, Zebra and Wildebeest graze on the long grass enabling the dainty impala and gazelle to nibble the smaller shoots. Close by, the predators, the lion and leopard, hyena and jackal lie ready to cull the weaklings from the herds and overhead vultures soar waiting to scavenge the remains—nothing is wasted in the great cycle of nature. Round the soda lakes millions of flamingoes, pink clouds reflected in the still water, offer a spectacle which alone makes the journey to Africa a unique experience.

EGYPT

The solid gold funeral mask of Tutankhamun *left* more than any other single item has brought to the world a new and continuing awareness of the remarkable civilisation that was ancient Egypt.

The wall paintings of the many tombs tell in graphic detail the story of ancient Egypt. Everyday events are depicted alongside the Gods and Goddesses in the strange funeral rites and rituals which obsessed the Ancient Egyptians.

Osiris, God of the Dead, *right* and Senendrem and his wife worshipping *far right* are seen in their tomb at Luxor.

Queen Nefertary, daughter-wife of Ramses the Great in her tomb at Luxor *right* and Anubis between Osiris and Horus in the Tomb of Horemheb *far right*.

Nefertiti *right* was the wife of Akhenaton, creator of the new religion, monotheism.

The Great Sphinx *right* keeps watch over the sacred area of the Pyramid of Chephron, one of the three great pyramids at Gizeh and the last remaining Wonder of the ancient world.

Ammon Re *above* Lord of Heaven, was the chief of the Gods of ancient Egypt.

The Temple of Abu Simbel *right* was threatened by drowning in the lake formed by the waters of the Aswan Dam. Now the 60 feet high statues of Ramses the Great have been elevated to a new position clear of the water.

A fish seller at Faiyum *below* and a marriage feast *bottom* taking place beneath the shade of a Bedouin tent.

Methods of agriculture and places of habitation have remained unchanged for centuries. Gebel Togo, *right* is a Nubian village at Aswan.

WEST AFRICA

The vast area of West Africa along the Gold Coast ranges from Senegal to Cameroun and Gabon; from the inland desert regions which fringe the Sahara to the rich coastal areas which include small states like Dahomey *right.* The many tribes which make up these countries are now, after much strife and with the unhappy inheritance of the slave trade from which the coast took its name, trying to weld themselves into nations with strong identities. The ports of Senegal and Sierra Leone are now being drawn into the ever increasing tourist business as they become ports of call for the many cruises from the Canary Isles off the Spanish Sahara coast.

MOROCCO

Morocco is the largest of the Barbary States and includes the Atlas Mountains. Old methods of agriculture are still used *right* and old traditions such as the veil for women still prevail *below* both in the country as well as the main towns such as Rabat and Casablanca. The tough desert Berbers *left* are skilled riders.

The cave dwellers of Matmata *left* and *below* have adapted to both the climate and terrain by digging square holes to just above the water level and live in caves around the sides of the square, thus ensuring a ready water supply and continual shelter from the sun.

Sousse is rapidly becoming an important holiday centre around the old village where the camel market *left* is still held.

KENYA

Kenya covers nearly a quarter of a million square miles of East Africa around the Equator. Most of the population is found in the highland areas and lives by agriculture.

Nairobi *above* is the capital of Kenya and was founded only in 1899.

The Masai people *left* have extensive grazing rights in the Amboselli National Park.

The varied wildlife of Africa can be seen *right* in the natural scenic splendour of the many National Parks across the continent.

SOUTH AFRICA

Cape Town *above* with its fine natural harbour and Table Mountain is the Republic's capital, as well as being the centre of the important wine trade. Pretoria is the administrative capital and was founded in 1855 by Pretorius, the first president of the old South African Republic.

The Government Buildings *left* are framed by jacaranda trees with which this elegant city abounds.

NORTH AMERICA

The ancient world was the nursery for the subraces of mankind and when the first men reached the new world of North America they were fully men. They were Mongoloid tribes whose daring wanderings took them, some fifteen thousand years ago, to the far north where the Bering Strait separates the two great land masses of Eurasia and America. Using skin and wattle coracles, similar to the boats still used on the west coast of Ireland, they crossed the icy waters to their new home. The most recent of these migrations were the Eskimo, who still use kayaks, a more sophisticated form of coracle. These tribes for the most part remained at a level of Neolithic barbarism, but some in isolation from the rest developed into the legendary American Indian, the Redskin. This 'noble savage' was a meat eater like the Eskimo and, like the Eskimo, had prodigious powers of endurance. He painted his body, wore feathers, built tepees and worshipped a god of creation. Fortunately for these remarkable people the animals they hunted for food and skins had arrived millions of years earlier when dry land joined the two continents. These animals in spite of their long existence in the country were still almost identical to their Eurasian fellows. The American buffalo to the European bison; the moose to the elk; the caribou to the reindeer, whilst the smaller animals, fox beaver, otter, bear the same names. Originally there had been a greater variety and deposits in the Miocene Age, which started twenty-five million years ago and lasted fourteen million years, show remains of several species of camels and llamas. The latter still survive in South America.

Modern discovery of America was made on 12th October, 1492 when the Spaniard, Christopher Columbus, made landfall on the Bahamas. He and his contemporaries believed the land he had reached to be the Eastern extremity of Asia, hence he called it the Indies. Like his early predecessors, Columbus had frail craft for his long voyage—two open boats of fifty tons each and the hundred-ton *Santa Maria* which was decked in. This little expedition of eighty-eight men sailed due west into an unknown sea for two months and nine days, wondering, no doubt, if they would ever see Spain or indeed land again. Our astronauts have the advantage of knowing where they are bound and how long it will take, to say nothing of being in constant contact with their home control. These courageous sailors dazzled Europe with their discovery and slowly the immense good fortune of Spain became apparent; she had found a new world abounding in gold and silver and she lost no time in exploiting the situation.

The first people encountered by the Spaniards in their rush for gold were of Mongoloid type whom the victors killed, robbed, enslaved and baptized. As the expeditions continued their advance into their new possessions they discovered a system of civilisation that had developed in America, probably independently of the civilisation of the old world; the Aztecs of Mexico. These people had a manner of living similar to that of the early Sumerian cities of pre-dynastic Egypt, but they were thousands of years behind the explorers who became their conquerors. The Aztecs had a way of life which depended on human sacrifice. This religion was like a ghastly caricature of the Old Testament. Their minds were haunted by the idea of sin and the need for bloody propitiations in which the usual method was to cut open the human victim with a stone knife and tear the still beating heart from his body. Unfortunately, very little is known about these fascinating people or their customs—the first invaders came for gold and failed to make records of these early Americans. Between 1519 and 1521 the Aztec civilisation was destroyed by a small expedition under Cortez and the possibility of learning more about it lost. The country became New Spain and so remained until the last viceroy was forced to resign when in 1821 the area became part of the United States.

The English, French and Dutch were also interested in acquiring part of the booty, but they were late starters on the treasure trail for foreign empires and it was not until 1584 that Sir Walter Raleigh set out to win British colonies in America. The first to be founded was Virginia, named after Elizabeth, the virgin Queen of England. A Quaker, Penn, founded the colony of Pennsylvania and a home for Catholics under the name of Maryland was made beside Virginia. At the same time in the north the Plymouth Company obtained a charter and began to settle in New England. The first ship to New England was the Mayflower and her passengers were Protestants hoping for more freedom in the new country. Unfortunately there was a difference in attitudes between the north and south and this was eventually to lead to civil war, but

meantime they were held together by their joint fears of the Indians, the French and the British.

The British had gradually gained control of their Dutch and French competitors by encouraging settlements and by 1750 they had a population of more than a million against the hundred thousand French. France had spread too rapidly through the great prairie plains, making treaties with the Indians, but failing to set up towns or forts to consolidate their interests. In 1759 the British and Colonial forces under General Wolfe took Quebec and in 1763 Canada was ceded to Britain. The French occupation was over except for Louisiana, named after Louis XIV, which remained outside British control. It was taken over by Spain in 1800, recovered by France and finally bought by the United States government in 1803. The American colonists learnt a great deal about war from the British and this was to be of value to them in the future.

The colonists were now much more securely established and in 1763, when King George III resolved to dominate and tax his American dominions, a strong resentment grew which led to a revolt against Britain and the War of Independence. This war started on 8th April, 1775 and ended almost eight years later on 19th April, 1783. From this followed a liberated and independent United States of America and by 1823 it was able to extend its policy of isolation to the rest of the old world from which it remained aloof until 1917 when the First Great War obliged it to re-enter world politics. America became a different civilisation, it had no monarch, no titled people claiming privilege as a right, it had no state religion and believed in social and political equality for all. 'All men are born equal' was its philosophy, but alas all men are not born equal, they carry with them the complex programming of their individual ancestors which enmesh them from birth to death. Women were not included in this equality and today still ask for equal rights.

The first step towards equality was to give every male adult taxpayer a vote so that the will of the people could be the guiding force. This ideal led to a clash between the slave-owning states of the south and the free industrial north. The majority of the people called for the abolition of slavery, for all men are not born equal if some are born slaves. On 4th March 1861 Abraham Lincoln was elected President with the Southern States already in active secession. On 12th April the Civil War began with the bombardment of Fort Sumter at Charlestown and, after four years of bloody fighting, ended on 2nd April 1865 with a victory for the north. Thirteen days later this great American lay dead from an assassin's bullet. His death slowed up the healing of the rift between North and South but the Union was saved. This great democracy was a new thing in the experience of the world and attracted multitudes of people who came to seek their fortune in a free country. In the seventeenth century half a million emigrated from Britain; in the eighteenth, three times that number came, mainly from Ireland and Scotland. From 1900 to 1920 seventeen million Europeans came to North America. This flood of people from different backgrounds, with an abundant variety of skills and crafts, now wedded to the vast resources of their new land, led to an industrial growth never before possible. Here was opportunity for all, hard work and industry brought personal reward, jack was as good as his master and everyone's dreams could be realised.

From such beginnings it is not surprising that America should be a land of man-made wonders. The most famous suspension bridge in the world—the Golden Gate Bridge in San Francisco; the New York skyline with the tallest buildings in the world; the huge telescope on Mount Palomar, the largest inland waterway—the St. Lawrence Seaway linking the Great Lakes with the Atlantic, the largest rocket launching site at Cape Canaveral—which put the first men on the moon and started man's ability to live in other worlds. In addition her natural wonders are superlative. The Grand Canyon—the longest and deepest gorge in the world, the Mammoth Caves of National Park, sixty thousand of them extending over an area of nine thousand square miles, the Yellowstone National Park and Niagara-Falls. There is much to marvel at in this new world.

GREENLAND

Greenland between the Arctic Ocean and Baffin Bay was first colonised by the Danes in 1721. It is a lofty ice-capped plateau peopled by coastal settlements of Eskimos. Over seven-eighths of the country is under a permanent ice-cap.
Whaling and walrus hunting form a major part of the country's industry.

CANADA

The Horseshoe Falls at Niagara *left* are much bigger than the American Rainbow Falls. They are 207 feet deep and over half a million cubic yards of water plunge over the edge every minute.

Confederation Square and Parliament Hill *below* in Ottawa, the federal capital.

Harvesting wheat *right* between Calgary and Letherbridge, Alberta. Canada's famous Royal Canadian Mounted Police *bottom right* pictured taking part in their musical ride.

Montreal *overleaf* is built on several islands in the St. Lawrence river and is the second largest French speaking city in the world. Following Montreal is a magnificent Panorama of the Banff National Park.

USA

Fifth Avenue *below left* is the major shopping street in New York.

Boston *below* is the main city of Massachusetts.

The Capitol, Washington *right* is the seat of Government.

The vast Rockefeller Centre complex *left* is the dominating feature of Fifth Avenue. It includes the famous Radio City Music Hall and from the topmost peak there is a remarkable panoramic view of New York *overleaf*.

Central Park is the major recreation centre of New York and in recent years has provided the home for free concerts, ice skating *right* and Sunday bicycling. It also has a zoo, lakes and riding stables. On its eastern side is the Metropolitan Museum of Art.

IN THIS TEMPLE
AS IN THE HEARTS OF THE PEOPLE
FOR WHOM HE SAVED THE UNION
THE MEMORY OF ABRAHAM LINCOLN
IS ENSHRINED FOREVER

The American dream come true perfectly captured in Vermont *left* as the dying leaves from the maple trees set alight the whole countryside surrounding the small farms and villages such as the Red House, Bennington *centre left*.

The serenity of St. Urbain Farm, Charlevoix, Michigan *left* is in direct contrast to the gambler's dream at Las Vegas *above* which blossoms in the desert by virtue of its artesian water supply. It is ironic to think that its first settlers were the Mormons.

Disneyland is a fantasy town just 45 minutes drive from Los Angeles. Built to recreate the world of Walt Disney pictures it is a place of pure escapism where parents and children can live out parts of their history and folk memories.

San Francisco is built on the San Andreas Fault, a thin fissure in the earth's crust, movement of which caused the partial destruction of the city in 1906 and further movements seem inevitable. Its streets climb sharply from the sea front with the famous cable cars lurching up them. Fisherman's Wharf is famous for its seafood restaurants. The world's longest bridge spans the Bay, but its fame is eclipsed by the more popular Golden Gate bridge *overleaf*.

NEW MEXICO

New Mexico lies north of the Mexican Republic and south of Colorado and is crossed by the Rocky Mountains. The Indian inhabitants still maintain their old traditions and ceremonies *this page* and their traditional enemies, the cowboys, are still the rough tough men immortalised in countless films and rodeos *opposite* are still one of the main attractions.

WEST INDIES

The many islands which make up the Caribbean offer the most comprehensive and at the same time the most luxurious of holiday worlds. The bay near Port Antonio at the northeast end of the island of Jamaica *below* is a typical example of the unspoiled scenery. Grande Anse Beach, Grenada, *right* is one of the finest in the Caribbean with shining sand stretching for over 2 miles.

Antigua Bay *top right* has splendid beaches and many famous historical monuments. The capital of this highly developed island is St. John's. Bridgetown *bottom right* is the capital of Barbados. With a strong English tradition the harbour police wear the uniform of Nelson's sailors and in Trafalgar Square there is a statue of Nelson 27 years older than that in London.

SOUTH AMERICA

South America covers 7,300,000 square miles and has a population of 175 million. The country varies from burning deserts and tropical forests to the icy isolation of Antarctica in the Southern Ocean. Like North America, there are no signs of early man in these regions, the first arrivals came from the north by way of the Central American Isthmus, though, no doubt, there were a few who may have drifted there on primitive rafts or boats. The Kon Tiki and Ra II expeditions of Thor Heyerdahl proved this possible.

Two civilisations were discovered by the European adventurers of the fifteenth century, the Maya of Yucatan and the Inca of Peru. Both are interesting because they preserved ideas and methods that had long since passed out of old-world experience. They had no iron, but worked in gold, silver and copper. They carved stone with great skill, made pots and were proficient weavers and dyers. Like the old world of 3000 B.C. they were governed by priest-kings and had ritual human sacrifices for seed and harvest times. Their priests were first class astronomers, better than their colleagues in the old world and Maya writing was largely devoted to keeping complicated calendars. These records were not only carved on stone, but also painted on skins. The people of Peru did not have writing, but kept their records by tying knots upon strings of different colours. Some of these string bundles called *quipus* have been discovered, but so far it has not been possible to interpret them. The Maya kingdom extended over the Mexican peninsula and the bordering land to the south. Some hundred and thirty of their ruined temples remain scattered through this area. One of the most famous is Chichen Itza. This massive ruined city was almost as large as the ruins of Angkor in Cambodia. The Temple of the Warriors is surrounded by a thousand pillars, now lying in ruins, and the people who inhabited them have vanished as mysteriously as did the city dwellers of Angkor.

The European discovery of South America began with a Portuguese sailor, Magellan, who followed the coast down to the strait named after him. Having passed through this forbidding stretch of water he continued to sail out into the Pacific Ocean for ninety-eight days. This was the beginning of the first voyage to circumnavigate the world and it says much for the courage of Magellan and his crew that they kept steadfastly on into that empty sea. Scurvy and sickness assailed the crew whose only food was brackish water and putrid biscuits, but Magellan sailed on and eventually the expedition, in a pitiful state, reached the Marianas. Still continuing, they discovered the Philippines and here the courageous Magellan was killed and other captains murdered. Still they sailed on until finally the *Vittoria* with a crew of thirty-one returned to Seville in July 1522. They were all that remained of the five ships that started in August 1519 with two hundred and eighty men, but they had proved, beyond doubt, that the world was a globe and from this moment on the sea lost the terror of the unknown.

In 1530 Pizarro sailed from the Isthmus of Panama with one hundred and sixty-eight Spaniards and captured the Inca of Peru, Atahualpa, by treachery. The Inca was held to ransom for 'enough gold to fill a room' which was duly delivered but, in spite of this, Atahualpa was murdered and his golden empire ruthlessly exploited by Pizarro and his soldiers. Soon the Inca empire was in his hands and Spanish adventurers spread rapidly over the rest of South America, with the exception of Brazil which had fallen to the Portuguese. One Inca stronghold however escaped, the city of Machu Picchu, high and lonely in the Central Andes. Machu Piccu means 'old peak' and this magnificent ruined city rests on a small plateau nine thousand feet above sea level. At one end of the flat space a conical mountain pierces the sky, but even its almost inaccessible sides are cut with neatly terraced fields. Aqueducts bring mountain spring water to the fountains which intersperse the complex of tombs and temples, terraces and staircases, all carved from granite, and archaeological treasure that the world flocks to see. The city is so remote that it lay undiscovered until 1911. It is thought to be the last refuge of the Inca King Manco and the final scene of a brilliantly organised civilisation. The Incas like the Ancient Egyptians worshipped the sun, the Giver of Life and the main feature of Machu Picchu is a massive, curiously carved stone that served as a sundial measuring the seasons and as an altar for appropriate sacrifices at seed time and harvest.

The Incas were the last god-kings of this world and developed independently of those of the ancient world. They show man's need for something beyond himself. All animals start life as dependents and few, including man, ever free themselves from the desire for leaders and protection.

Following the Spanish and Portuguese invaders came the church. Much of their teaching at this

time was influenced by a young monk, Ignatius Loyala, who in 1539 founded the 'Society of Jesus'. This order carried Christianity to India and China and their missionaries were the chief workers in South America where they had a strong civilizing influence on the now leaderless inhabitants. The Jesuit schools were, and still are, famous throughout the world and they taught the natives crafts and skills as well as Christianity. Their impact on the country is seen in the beautiful cathedrals that adorn all the principal cities as well as the simple churches of the villages. With the exception of the remote forest Indian tribes, who still continue their primitive way of life, wary of the outside world, the majority of the population have intermarried with the immigrants and produced a great variety of blood strains. In Rio de Janeiro one can see people of every colour mingling happily in what is claimed to be the most beautiful city in the world. The name came when on 20th January 1590 the Portuguese mistook the bay for the mouth of a river and named it after the month—'January River.' The view from the Corcovada mountain shows the vast bay studded with islands–sunlight glittering on the blue water and silver beaches. Towering above the mountain summit stands the eighty feet high figure of Christ, arms outstretched above the bustle of the four million citizens.

Like North America the colonies of South America threw off the dominion of foreign powers and became republics in their own rights in the early nineteenth century. Only three European colonies remained to the twentieth century, British, French and Dutch Guinea and these are now self-governing. The colonists who came to South America were different from the North American who sought for conditions similar to Europe. In South America they came first because of the wealth of gold and silver, but stayed to produce copper, nitrates and to supply the world with huge quantities of meat, coffee and cocoa. As trade opened up, the idea of a canal linking the Atlantic and Pacific oceans through the Isthmus of Panama became of increasing importance. It had first been considered in 1524, but it was not until 1879 that work on the project began, when the USA acquired sole rights to build it. Seven years were spent on moving mountains of debris and fifty-six thousand workers died of malaria and yellow fever. On 15th June 1920 the waterway was opened to the ships of the world. This modern wonder is forty miles long and raises and lowers ships eighty-five feet on each passage. The Iguacu Falls, a natural wonder, more than equals the man-made wonder of the Panama Canal. It is the grandest waterfall in the world;

seven times the volume of Niagara. One hundred and forty million tons of water an hour pour over the one and a half miles of falls plunging into a narrow gorge two hundred and fifty feet below. The falls are at a remote spot where three countries meet, Brazil, Argentina and Paraguay on the river Iguacu, a tributary of the 2,900 mile long Parama which joins the River de la Plata to flow into the Atlantic at Buenos Aires.

One can expect something remarkable from this free mixture of races of South America and perhaps a significant milestone was the decision of the government of Brazil to build a new capital unique in the history of the world. The first discussions to move the capital from Rio de Janeiro to the interior, took place in 1825 and, after a long period of gestation building began in 1956. The new capital grew on empty land and was designed to escape completely from the sprawl of other cities. Oscar Niemeyer the architect worked with almost unlimited freedom. His plan was in the form of a cross, three and a half miles long and three hundred and seventy yards wide, with a bow shaped crosspiece. The huge avenue formed by the length of the cross would provide for public buildings, whilst the bow would contain living complexes comprising, flats, schools, churches, business premises and recreation areas. Everything was included in the original plan—university, theatres, hotels, hospitals and swimming pools. On 21st April 1960 Brazilia was opened on schedule and today there are more than three hundred thousand people living there. A new city for a new world.

ECUADOR

Ecuador encompasses both the heights of the Andes and the Galapagos Islands with their astonishing plant and animal life. Its capital Quito *left* and *below* is on the site of the ancient capital of the Incas at the foot of the volcano Pichincha and is one of the best preserved Spanish colonial towns with its finely decorated cathedral *overleaf.*

PERU

Peru is the third largest country in South America. Its capital Lima is served by the port of Callao *above* on the Pacific coast and is now the centre of the important fishmeal industry. It was founded by Pizarro in 1533 after he had finally defeated the Incas.

Incas who survived the brutal defeats by Pizarro retreated to mountain strongholds such as Machu Picchu *left* which lay hidden until 1911. Built on solid rock it has over 3,500 steps and was thought to have housed over 10,000 people.

The population of Peru is mostly pure-bred Indian *below* with the remainder being of mixed or pure Spanish descent. The country is strongly Roman Catholic and there are many religious festivals and processions of relics *right*.

The ancient Inca capital of Cuzco, *bottom* now a market town, contains many ancient relics of the great Inca palaces and the Temple of the Sun, –the centre of Inca religious life.

ARGENTINA

Argentina occupies most of the southern half of South America and is nearly as large as Western Europe. It stretches from the Tropic of Capricorn to Tierra del Fuego near Antarctica. Buenos Aires is the capital, lying at the mouth of Rio de la Plata 'River of Silver.' It is an important commercial and shipping centre and its very modern buildings are mingled with fine old ones such as the Congress Buildings *top right* and on the outskirts the brightly coloured Boca houses *below* which achieve a pop-art effect without effort.

La Paz is the capital of Bolivia and is the site of much pre-Inca civilisation. The population is over half pure Indian who still retain their traditional dress and on Lake Titicaca *bottom* still use woven reed-boats remarkably similar to those in use in Ancient Egypt. The recent Ra expedition set out to prove that they could indeed have originated in Egypt.

The Iguacu Falls *overleaf* between Paraguay and Brazil are seven times the size of Niagara in volume of water. 21 falls plunge over nearly two miles of cliffs.

IGUACU FALLS

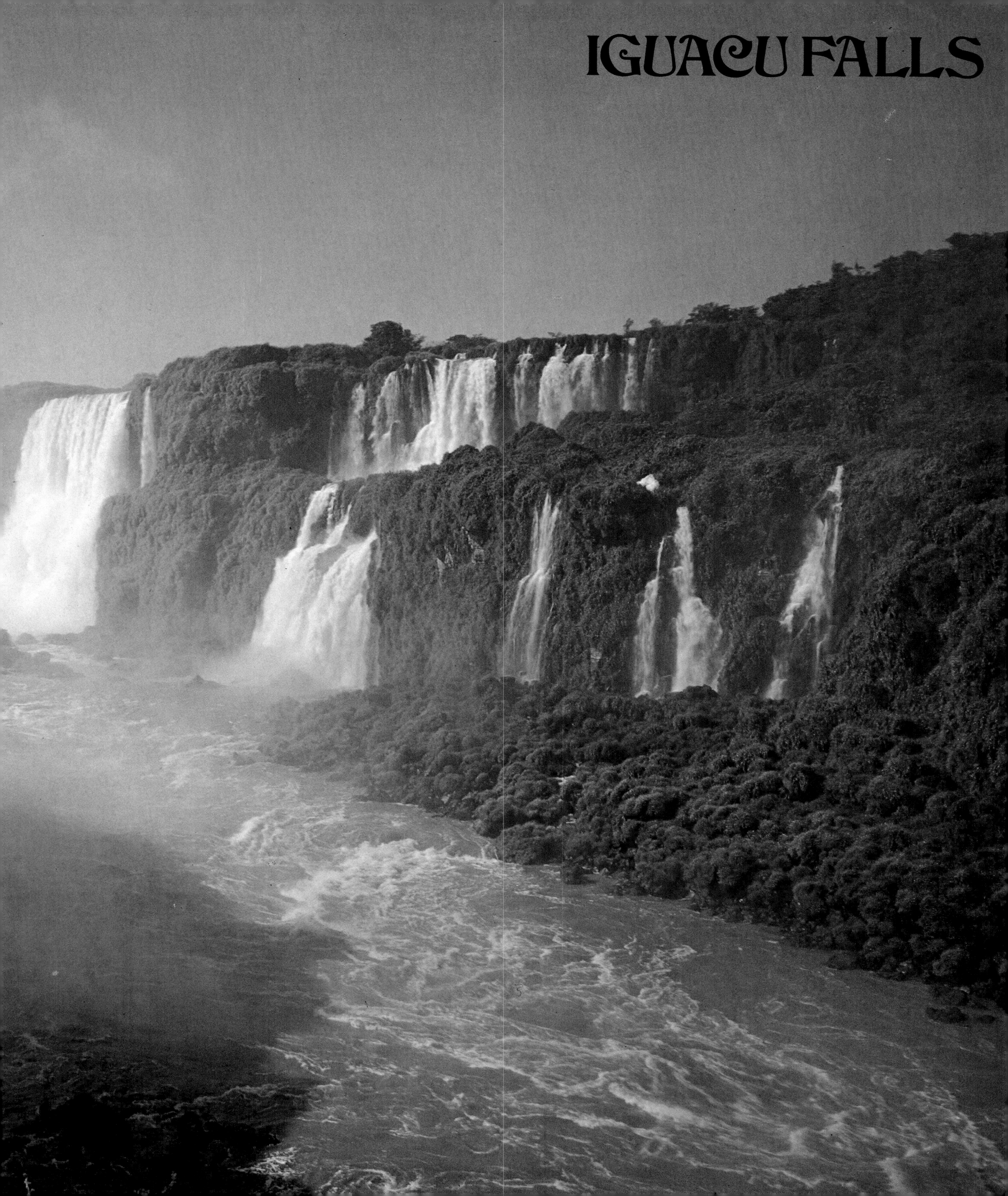

MEXICO

High in central Mexico stands the capital, Mexico City, from which can be seen the majestic peak of the volcano Popocatapetl. In the same square as the National Palace, *left* once the seat of the Spanish viceroys and now the seat of the Federal Government, stands the Cathedral, the oldest Christian building in the Americas.

Acapulco *left* is the chief coastal resort, its 60 hotels and motels catering for everyone from the international jet-set to those with modest tastes.

Chichen Itza *left* is a major Aztec temple with both Mayan and Toltec influences. The Temple of Warriors is surrounded by over 1000 pillars and the Sacred Pyramid lies at the centre. There is also a pitch for the sacred game of Pelota.

Between the Pacific and the Andes lies the narrow ribbon of country which is Chile, over 2,600 miles long and not much more than 100 miles wide. It has been independent of Spain since 1810 and is the fourth largest state in South America.

BRAZIL

The buildings of Brazil range from tiny mountainside villages to the elegant city of Rio de Janiero with its sugarloaf mountain *above* and the ultra-modern new capital of Brasilia *left* standing on the shores of a lake.
Rio offers all the pleasures of a cosmopolitan city with its flowery parks and gracious old buildings as well as those of a holiday resort with its splendid beach at Copacabana *above right*, its bars, hotels and nightclubs and the famous carnivals *right* which together with coffee sum up Brazil for most people.

EURASIA and the Far East

Eurasia covers a third of the world's land area and contains nearly half its population, the majority of whom are Chinese. These remarkable people possess a civilisation that has survived to the present day, from 2500 B.C. The earliest human remains so far discovered in this area are those of the famous Peking and Landien men some half a million years old. Later discoveries of stone implements, tools and pottery, dating from about 10,000 B.C. show the beginnings of an agricultural society in the valley of the Yellow River. The Chinese are still agriculturalists and it says much for their skill that they have been able to grow their main crop of rice on the same fields for thousands of years. They were the first conservationists and were careful to return to their land all the organic fertiliser available, including that supplied by man, a custom that is still in force and one that western anti-pollutionists might profitably consider.

As well as being good husbandmen, the Chinese were inventors and artists. They gave the world the wheel, the magnetic compass, gunpowder and exquisite works in jade, bronze, ivory and terracotta, as well as beautiful silks and brocades. Fresh treasures are still being found, the latest being two magnificent death suits for a prince and princess of the Han Dynasty. They were made of plaques of jade fastened together with gold thread, designed to protect the bodies in a similar manner to the mummy cases of Ancient Egypt. In addition to material treasure, the Chinese were well supplied with wisdom and as early as the fifth century B.C. had the good fortune to receive the teachings of Buddha, Laotze, and Confucius, who all lived at this time. These eminent philosophers spoke of gentleness and justice and not of terrible deities, demons or heavenly hereafters. Modern Chinese have no interest in a paradise to come, but apply themselves diligently to making their country free from poverty, disease, robbery and violence in which endeavour they have met with considerable success. Perhaps of more interest to the west is their success in using their ancient system of acupuncture for obtaining anaesthesia for surgery. Slim needles are placed beneath the patient's skin and enable major surgery to be performed without pain. The ability of the patient to talk to the surgeon and the elimination of the after effects of drug anaesthesia are valuable and there is the added advantage that this method does not require heavy and expensive equipment to be sent to outlying areas of this vast country.

Apart from the small delicate objects, so beautifully produced, the Chinese are responsible for the largest man made structure in the world. In bulk it equals one hundred and twenty pyramids the size of the Great Pyramid of Cheops and stretches for one thousand five hundred miles from the steppes of Central Asia to the Yellow Sea. It is the Great Wall of China, the only man made object which can be seen from another planet. Building commenced 2,600 years ago and was completed in the Ming Dynasty, 1368-1643. It was to protect China from the barbarians and certainly up to now the people have been little influenced by the world outside. But there are signs that the old barriers may be coming down and it is to be hoped that the world may benefit from exchanges with this remarkable country.

The second largest country in Eurasia is the subcontinent formed by Pakistan and India. Here, hidden amongst the towering ice-capped peaks of the Pakistan Himalayas lie fertile valleys whose inhabitants have been isolated for centuries from the tensions and haste of modern life. These small communities of moslems (settled in areas round Chitral, Gilgit and Hunza), grow some of the finest fruit in the world, tend their flocks of half-sized cattle, sheep and goats and play polo, a game which they invented. They also live to great ages in their 'Shangri La' existence surrounded by scenery of unequalled beauty and serenity. Pakistan was also the site of the fierce battles of legendary figures such as Alexander the Great, Mahmud of Ghazni, Barbar and Akbar the Great. The historic Khyber Pass has been, throughout history the most important gateway from Central Asia to the subcontinent. Through it came Greeks who combined with the Buddhists to produce the great traditions of Graeco-Buddhist art, so evident in the museums of Pakistan. At Lahore and Thatta exquisite forts and palaces, mosques and tombs, gardens and pavilions bear witness to the Mogul Emperors who dreamed like poets and who built like lions. The highly developed Indus Valley Civilisation, comparable to the great cities of Egypt and Mesopotamia five thousand years ago, may be seen at Harappa and Mohenjo-Daro. Alas these cities had no great wall to protect them and their civilisation, like their mud and brick built houses, was swept away by barbarian hordes. Although their material prosperity was shattered, part of their spiritual thought survived to provide the most sensuous religion known to man. This grew out of nature worship and fertility rites and created an astounding complexity of exotic and aesthetic painting and sculpture. No one who has made the journey to the rock-hewn temples of Ajanta and Ellora, or the temples of Madurai and Khajuraho can fail to be impressed by the centuries-old saturation of religious feeling which pervades everything, the air one breathes, the stones one treads. It lingers in the quiet movement of the scented leaves and in the shimmering haze of heat beyond their shadow. India beyond all doubt is a land intoxicated with religion. Twined in voluptuous attitudes of love the Devadasi, temple prostitutes, slave girls of the gods, display their charms in melting forms of stone. Love has always been the central theme of life here and nowhere is it portrayed more clearly than in the most beautiful tomb on earth, the Taj Mahal. Built by the Moslem Emperor Shah Jahan in 1631 for his lovely wife Mumtaz-i-Mahal, 'Jewel of the Palace', it is without equal, a dream of white marble, its exquisite beauty reflected in the still water that leads to the entrance.

Adjoining eastern India, high up in the Himalayas lies the tiny kingdom of Nepal, where Buddha was born about 563 B.C. From the temple of Svayambunath in Katmandu his painted eyes gaze out upon the four corners of the earth contemplating the odd ability of mankind to translate his simple message into fabulous realms of deities and demons housed in gorgeous shrines and temples. Further east the most exotic of these adorn the glittering city of Bangkok. From the gaily coloured multi-tiered roofs of the gold-encrusted temples hang thousands of little bells, their clappers fashioned like the leaves of the Bodhi tree beneath which the Buddha found enlightenment. The slightest breeze moves them into gentle sounds to welcome the visitor on his pilgrimage. Through the courtyards and gaily painted colonnades ancient monks and their disciples move gracefully in their yellow robes, gravely regarding the travellers who have come to watch or worship. As one moves through the sunlit scene it is interesting to reflect that not only the great religions, Christianity, Buddhism, Hinduism and Islam, but also the smaller, Judaism, Parseeism, Taoism and Shintoism, all had their origins in the east.

In nearby Cambodia the huge temple of

Angkor Wat, a cool grey miracle of stone, rises out of the dense green jungle. The walls form a canvas more than half a mile in length every inch of which is covered with deeply carved scenes from the two great Indian Epics, the Ramayana and the Mahabharata. Battles rage between demons and gods, elephants trample victims of spear and arrow. The fight continues on water and war canoes with snake-headed prows thrust savagely at one another, while the fighting men attack with sword and lance. Unfortunate losers flounder in the water where crocodiles devour them. To the south west lies the lovely island of Ceylon. Here in the ruined city of Anauradhapura stands a living link with the past. It is a Bo tree grown from a cutting of the original tree under which Buddha found enlightenment. Now over 2,300 years old this venerable growth must be the oldest historical tree in existence.

Farthest east of all stands the Great Buddha of Kamakura in Japan. The bronze cast weighing 210,000 pounds was erected in 1252. From an imposing height of forty-two feet the colossal figure looks down with impenetrable calm upon the multitudes that come to see him. The half closed eyes and the meditative pose represent the incarnation of compassion, the spiritual principle of Buddha. Much of the outlook of Eurasia is influenced by the philosophy of Buddha which is now becoming popular in the west. Buddha was not a god, but the wealthy son of a minor king in Nepal. Highly intelligent, he sought an answer to the problems of living, not like the Ancient Egyptians, concerned with creating another world, but simply a solution for dealing with life as he found it. Meditating for six years, in lonely places, he finally found enlightenment in Bodh Gaya near Benares. He recognised that ignorance is the root of all evil, that the cause of sorrow is hidden in the ignorance from which life grows—the child is born a savage. His fundamental teaching is that the suffering and misery of humanity arise from insatiable selfishness and unlimited craving for personal satisfaction. The man who escapes from the tyranny of his ego occupying the centre of his private thoughts becomes free. It is perhaps significant that while mighty empires built on greed and aggression have never lasted more than a few centuries, the selfless life of the Buddhist community has carried it safely through 2,500 years. The meek have, indeed, inherited the earth.

In recent years a remarkable number of archaeological discoveries have been made in China, none more spectacular than the treasures from the Han Tombs, dating from B.C., such as the Servant with a Lamp *left* and the Jade Burial Suit of Princess Tou Wan *right*.

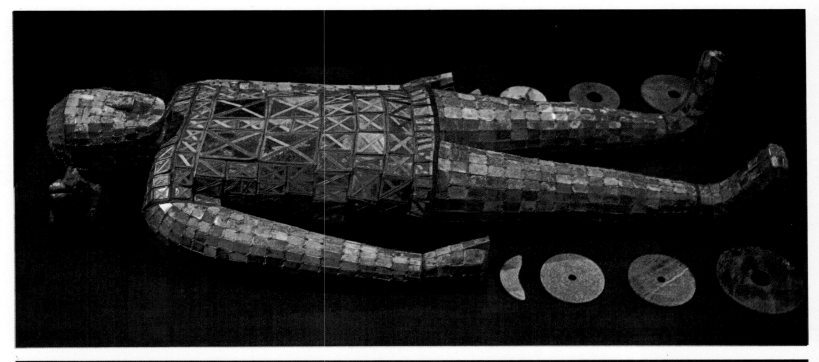

The bronze horses *right* are typical of those from the Tomb of Leitai.

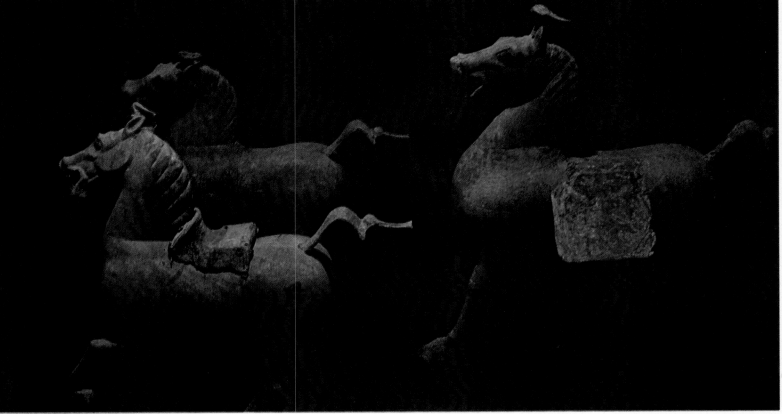

The Forbidden City *right* was the home of the Emperors and is now open to all the people.

The Great Wall of China *overleaf* is over 1500 miles long and 16 feet wide at the top. It is the only man-made building visible from the moon.

Chinese children *left* celebrate May Day.

Bicycles are universally used in China and the bicycle park in Peking *left* is one of many for the thousands who cycle into the city each day.

The children *below* belong to a desert farm near Peking which is now, with modern methods, beginning to produce harvests.

NEPAL

Nepal lies in the Himalayas and includes Mount Everest. The people are made up of several different races with distinctive costumes, dialects and customs. Most of them are Hindu *bottom right* although there are many Buddhists. Agriculture is the main occupation producing cattle, rice and *right* corn, seen drying in a market at Bhadagon, centre of pottery and weaving. Katmandu, the capital *below* was founded in 723 and is said to have more temples and shrines than any other city. In the centre of the city is the main square with the Royal Palace and the Wooden Temple said to have been built from the wood of one tree from which the city takes its name.

At the high 8th century
fortress of Chittorgarh
top left is the Temple of
Fame and *top right*
worshippers relax in the
shade of a giant boulder
after prayers at the Temple
of Mahabilipuram in
South India.

The Punjab is the home of
the Sikhs, a 16th century
sect which has produced
fine warriors. Their most
sacred shrine *previous page*
is the Golden Temple at
Amritsar.

Hyderabad is the capital
of the state of Andhra
Pradesh on the Bay of
Bengal. Founded at the
end of the 16th century
it has many splendid
sights including *left*
the High Court.

Agra In Uttar Pradesh was
Mogul Akbar's capital in
the 16th century and it was
his grandson, Shah Jehan,
who built the Taj Mahal
right for his wife Mumtaz-i-
mahal 'Jewel of the Palace.'

New Delhi was designed by
Sir Edward Lutyens and was
formally opened in 1931 as
the seat of government. Its
impressive stone buildings
including the Secretariat
overleaf are a grandiose
reminder of British rule.

On the banks of the Ganges
many shrines, temples and
palaces rise in tiers, as at
Benares *left* and the ghats
(steps) are crowded as
pilgrims immerse them-
selves in the holy river.

Religion and ritual are an
integral part of the daily life
of the people both young
and old *below* and strange
rituals such as snake
charming *right* emphasise
the age-old significance of
the snake, which appears in
the religions of Ancient
Greece and Egypt.

JAVA

Java *below* has many mountains, some of them volcanic, and is densely populated. Intensively cultivated, the paddy fields sometimes completely encircle the villages.

CEYLON SRI LANKA

Sri Lanka, the resplendent land, has great contrasts; soaring mountains and deep lush valleys, glorious beaches and rushing rivers. There are coconut trees and giant banyan as well as the sacred Bo tree *right*, the oldest living historical tree, and said to be a cutting of the tree under which Buddha contemplated. Pan leaves are sold in the markets *far right* to wrap betel nuts for chewing.

Ceylon dates back to the 6th century B.C. when the Sinhalese 'the Lion people' settled in the island. Their ancient capital was Anaradhapura *right* once a thriving city of which only the stone foundations now stand like some ancient temple.

Rivers flow from the central mountain complex watering the tea plantations on the slopes and the rubber estates and paddy fields *right*.

PAKISTAN

The Indus Valley gave rise to one of the earliest known civilisations and at Mohenjodaro *below* there is a large well-planned city. The architecture of the Great Bath with the Citadel in the background is reflected in the stark modern architecture *bottom* of the Government Buildings at the new capital, Islamabad.

Alongside enormous modern advances old traditions still survive. The Dye seller in Lahore *below* supplies the important weaving trade. The food is always highly flavoured and the aromatic sweetmeats *below right* are best taken with a cup of local green tea.

Lahore is Pakistan's second city and has many fine buildings and gardens including the poetic Shalimar Terraces laid out by Shah Jehan and *bottom* the Mausoleum of the Emperor Jehangir.

AFGHANISTAN

The tough mountain people of Afghanistan are noted as exceptional warriors and their ferocity has been demonstrated in famous battles in the Khyber Pass *below* entered through the Kabul Gorge.

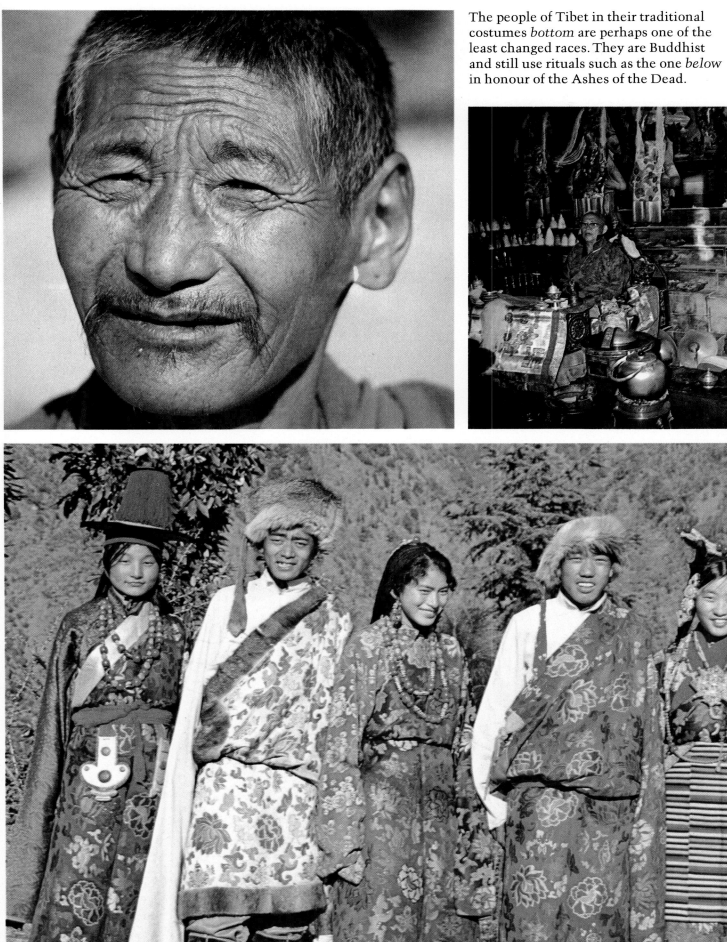

The people of Tibet in their traditional costumes *bottom* are perhaps one of the least changed races. They are Buddhist and still use rituals such as the one *below* in honour of the Ashes of the Dead.

THAILAND

The traditions of the arts of Thailand date back to 6th century India, with the music being older still. Thai dancers *above* are noted for their beauty and subtlety. Buddhism 6 centuries older than Christianity is the principal religion and most Thai males are especially religious, many spending three months as lay priests. The monks *left* are waiting to take part in a ceremony at Wat Phra Keo *right* the temple which contains the Emerald Buddha.

Bangkok is known as the
Venice of the East. The
floating market *below* is a
maze of waterways lined by
houses on wooden stilts and
supplies all those delicacies
and silks for which Thailand
is famous.

Singapore is an island republic off the
south of Malaya. First started as a trading
post in 1819 it nevertheless has an ancient
history and is now a major commercial
centre.

One of its successful businessmen,
creator of Tiger Balm, conceived a dream
world of heaven and hell depicting *left* in
colourful and surrealistic detail the
tortures of souls and the more fantastic
aspects of Chinese mythology. Away
from the modern city street markets
above continue unchanged.

HONG KONG

The bustling streets of Hong Kong *left* reflect the energy of this most vibrant city. A tiny corner of the Chinese mainland, it sparkles with life and commerce, but at night the neon-lit streets do not flash on and off as elsewhere, so close is the airport. While every aspect of Western culture and commerce is assimilated with ease traditional life continues.

The view of Hong Kong and Kowloon from The Peak is spectacular; the waters are busy with every type of ship from junk to ocean liner. The people who fill Hong Kong's bustling streets *bottom left* are nearly all Chinese made up of the Cantonese land dwellers and the Tanka boat dwellers who are the dominant seafarers of South China. About one-third of the population are refugees from China.

Some of the many and varied aspects of Hong Kong are shown *overleaf*.

JAPAN

Japan is made up of four main islands which form an arc enclosing the Sea of Japan. Its great cities appear totally westernised, yet throughout the country old standards of courtesy still operate.

The Ginza district of Tokyo *right* is the most lively part of the city.

Schoolchildren visit the Shinto Dazaisa Shrine, Fukuoka City, South Japan *below*.

Nakimase Street *below* with its colourful shops is in the Asakusa district of Tokyo.

Students of Tokyo College practice Judo *below* which has developed from Ju-Jitsu, one of the ancient martial arts and the official sport of Japan.

The Geysers at Ohwakunadi *bottom*, like those in New Zealand, are visited for both scenic splendour and medicinal effect.

Away from the cities, the old Japan *overleaf* reasserts itself.

AUSTRALASIA and the PACIFIC

The Pacific Ocean has an area of more than sixty-seven million square miles, nearly half the world's surface. From the Bering Strait to the Antarctic it measures nine thousand five hundred miles and at its widest point ten thousand. It has an average depth of fourteen thousand feet, descending to a staggering thirty-seven thousand eight hundred near the Marianas where Magellan made landfall after his perilous crossing. Sprouting from this vast sea are thousands of volcanic islands some still active in the Tonga Group, Hawaii, New Zealand and the Solomons. Now and then new islands appear when submerged volcanoes erupt, and treat the world once more to the spectacle of earlier times when mountains of white hot lava rose from steaming seas to form dry land. All life began in the sea and one of its most prolific forms is still with us, the coral polyp. This tiny blob of blind jelly no larger than a pin head is a primitive organism with only three moving parts. A mouth to take in food and expel waste, tentacles with stinging cells to paralyse and catch its victims and a body cavity in which the skeleton is formed with limy excretions extracted from the sea. These frail creatures can only survive in warm sunlit water with a high concentration of salt and perish at depths of one hundred and eighty feet. In spite of this they are responsible for nature's largest building—the Great Barrier Reef which extends along the east coast of Australia for one thousand two hundred and fifty miles with an astounding area of eighty thousand square miles. For millions of years the coral polyp patiently laboured to prepare a paradise for man. The dream islands of the South Pacific, the coral atoll with slim green coconut palms swaying over the limpid water of a lagoon formed in the crater of the dead volcano on which the polyps built with such effect. At low tide the living coral emerges from the blue sea revealing a magic carpet patterned with pools and shallows where brightly coloured fish flash amongst the strange shapes and hues contrived by these tireless builders. In deeper parts turtles, octopuses, moray eels, scorpion and stone fish with poisonous spines, sharks and barracuda patrol their districts ignoring the giant clams in their fixed stations. In the distance huge breakers thunder on the reef but fail to breach the bastion of skeletons.

For thousands of years the only inhabitants of these beautiful islands were exotic birds, animals and reptiles, many long extinct. Some remain to surprise us—the kiwi with feathers like coarse hair and unworkable wings, the kangaroo which carries its young in a pouch and moves in leaps, the duck-billed platypus and the spiny ant-eater both animals, but the only mammals known to man which do not give birth to their young but instead lay eggs. The first men to reach these islands were Pre-Dravidian types from South India and Negritoes, small negro people from Malayao-Polynesian regions. Similar people still survive; the Sakai of Malaya and the Veddas of Ceylon. Some may have come by way of the East Indies when there was possibly a land bridge to Australia, others island hopping on rafts and dugouts. The main settlements of the Negritoes were in Tasmania and Australia. They were nomads, expert hunters and trackers, typical of the Early Stone and Wood Age. Their stone implements were very crude, their weapon the wood spear which they used for hunting and fishing from their rafts of rolled up bark. They were naked except for skins thrown over their backs and a coating of grease decorated with red ochre and powdered charcoal to keep out the rain. These strange Palaelolithic people did not survive the impact of European civilisation, the cultural gap was too big to be bridged and even today similar extinction seems inevitable for the world's aboriginal tribes.

The discovery of Australia is claimed by Chinese and Malays—Marco Polo may have seen the country, but the first Europeans to land were the Dutch. In 1606 Captain Janz put some of his crew ashore at Cape Keerweer but they were attacked by the natives and sailed away. It was left to the formidable Captain Cook in his 370 ton Endeavour to take possession of the country for Britain on 28th April 1770—hoisting the Union Jack at Botany Bay. In 1778 a British colony was founded at Port Jackson, a penal station for criminals from England. In twelve years the convicts who numbered three quarters of the thirty thousand population had opened up the country with many roads and bridges. Sheep farming was introduced and in 1852 the wool clip amounted to forty-five million pounds. Copper and gold were found and soon immigrants from Europe, America and China were pouring in at the rate of two thousand a week. Adventurous men from all over the world still seek fortunes in this vast island; the latest being the opal miners. At Coober Pedy in the middle of arid desert lies the richest opal field in the world where three thousand people live underground like moles, sheltering from the heat, dust and flies as they toil in their workings. Those who strike lucky may emerge millionaires, a bucket full of opal rock can be worth a hundred thousand dollars. In far off Sydney a different treasure has risen from the ground, the famous Opera House, the only building of its kind in the world. Like the sails of some great ship filling with the wind of the future it carries the people of Australia forward upon another phase of their adventurous history.

Twelve hundred miles east of Australia, New Zealand also waited for man until recent times. In the fourteenth century Polynesians reached its northern shores and in 1642 Captain Abel Jansen Tasman found them there and gave the island the name it still bears. Ngauruhoe, 9,175 feet high, is still an active volcano and innumerable pools of boiling mud and water attract tourists and provide cures for various ailments. Five thousand miles further east giant stone statues gaze out to sea across the wind swept grass of Easter Island. This tiny volcanic island contains a mystery, an army of stone men, some over sixty feet high, naked except for the belts and huge hats which some still wear. They were once set up on platforms for worship miles away from the rock outcrop from which they were cut with stone picks. Thousands of tons of rock have been patiently severed from the mountain and half-finished figures still cling to the rock face. Nothing remains to tell for what purpose this gigantic task was undertaken. Religions in the Pacific vary greatly, an infinite number of cults and taboos exist from the mysterious rites of the aborigines with their sacred objects of wood and stone—a world of magic shared with the animals of whom they were most intelligent observers, to spirit worship sometimes suggesting a creator deity.

North of Australia in the highlands of New Britain, an island of the New Guinea Group, live a primitive tribe the Bainings of whom less than four thousand survive. From infancy they are taught to fear the wrath of their dead ancestors and this is emphasised in the ritual dances when grey clay daubed masks of terrifying appearance are worn by the spirit dancers. In nearby Java religion takes a gentler turn in the Temple of Borobudur, mountain of the gods, the vast monument built to Buddha during the 8th century A.D. It rises to a height of 115 feet in five square terraces, symbolising renunciation of worldly desires, of malevolence and malicious joy, of indolence and doubt, leading to the summit of inner peace and tranquility. Buddhist philosophy extended to many of the islands including Bali which is world famous for its tranquility and the grace and manners of its people. Whilst philosophy plays a large part in these matters the friendly embrace of the warm and bountiful sea must be given due credit. Tales of survival abound in the Pacific. Pitcairn Island, less than two miles long by a mile wide, still houses the last descendents of the mutineers of the Bounty who were exiled there two centuries ago. The latest people to benefit from nature's largesse were a young couple whose yacht foundered after an encounter with a forty foot whale. They escaped in two inflatable liferafts and lived for an incredible hundred and seventeen days on raw fish, turtle and sea birds. Their only drink was rainwater and the blood of their catches. The rubber skins of their rafts were constantly holed by spiny fish and sharks—only constant patching, inflating and bailing kept them afloat until a Korean fishing boat rescued them a hundred miles off the coast of Panama.

Finally to end our journey round this space ship which is our planet let us call at the most alluring island of them all—Tahiti. The very name echoes the magical power that captivated artists like Gauguin and writers like Robert Louis Stevenson, whose house still remains beneath the palms close to the endless breakers on the black volcanic sand. Charles Darwin came as a young scientist on the Beagle and some two centuries ago the first Europeans arrived, the men who sailed with Wallis, Bougainville and Cook. They saw the gleaming greens of the shore and lagoon, the white breakers roaring in from the blue of deep water. They landed in a paradise of innocence and plenty and were welcomed and loved by the most easy going and happy people in the world, whom even the most dedicated missions never succeeded in dominating. Everywhere flowers and fruit abound, hibiscus, bougainvillea, named by the captain, scented frangipani, coconuts, mangoes, durians, breadfruit, avocado, banana, mangosteen and papaya, free and unlimited food for the taking. Much of the old charm remains today, even with an endless stream of visitors, a way of life that challenges the stress and bustle of western civilisation, an island in a pattern of islands where people take their measure from nature and enjoy the banquet of life.

Hawaii in the Pacific is actually the 50th state of the United States of America, 2000 miles out into the ocean from the coast of California. The surfing *right* is world famous.

At Sea Park, Honolulu *below*, a killer whale leaps out of the water for food and dolphins skip over a rope of flowers held by the whale and an attractive instructress.

SAMOA

Samoa, like Tahiti, has attracted artists and travellers. It was discovered by the Dutch and visited by Louis de Bourgainville after whom the flower was named. Children dance in traditional dress *above* and swim in a mountain stream *left* and *right* Lefagu Beach in Western Samoa.

INDONESIA

Indonesia is a republic in South East Asia. The principal islands are Sumatra and Java, although Bali is undoubtedly most famous.

n Bali a funeral takes place *bove* complete with large udience and ritual burning.

he temple dancers of Bali *ight* are world famous for their ances in the old classical style. Deriving from Indian dances heir dramas are highly oloured and demand training rom early childhood.

177

AUSTRALIA

Australia is the world's largest island, although it is usually classed as a continent. The small island of Tasmania was the first part discovered and the land remained unclaimed until 1770 when Captain Cook anchored his ship in Botany Bay. The first settlers were convicts and the whole of Eastern Australia was designated a colony of Great Britain.

Sydney *overleaf* is the oldest and largest city and is the capital of New South Wales. Victorian buildings mix with modern skyscrapers and now the controversial Opera House *below* has been added to the sights. Although the majority of Australians are city dwellers they are also some of the most conscientious followers of the cult of the sun. Around Sydney there are many fine beaches such as Coogee *right* and the most famous at Bondi.

42

way he grips the edge of his desk when

pered. It took her forever to decide on

sorrow?

the wallpaper, she
told me. We stood
there, dwarfed by wall-
paper imprinted with
the trunks of shiny sil

—ANN BEATTIE

Escape LADDER

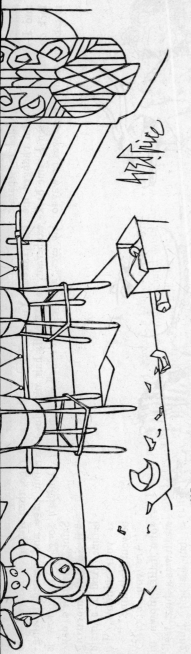

"I figured you were home. My soufflé just fell."

only lucky, we stared at the Schwitters show for one hour and twenty minutes, and then lunched. Vitello tonnato, as I recall.

When Herman was divorced in Boston . . . Carol got the good barbeque pit. I put it in the Blazer for her. In the back of the Blazer were cartons of books, tableware, sheets and towels, plants, and, oddly, two dozen white carnations fresh in their box. I pointed to the flowers. "Herman," she said, "he never gives up."

In Barcelona the lights went out. At dinner. Candles were produced and the shiny langoustines placed before us. Why do I love Barcelona above most other cities? Because Barcelona and I share a passion for walking? I was happy there? You were with me? We were celebrating my hundredth marriage? I'll stand on that. Show me a man who has not married a hundred times and I'll show you a wretch who does not deserve God's good world.

Lunching with the Holy Ghost I praised the world, and the Holy Ghost was pleased. "We have that little problem in Barcelona," He said. "The lights go out in the middle of dinner." "I've noticed," I said. "We're working on it," He said. "What a wonder-

ful city, one of our best." "A great town," I agreed. In an ecstasy of admiration for what is we ate our simple soup.

Tomorrow, fair and warmer, warmer and fair, most fair. . . .

—DONALD BARTHELME

•

None can be sure that having won an engine contract for a new jet aircraft, it will not be lost when a competitor comes up with a better mousetrap.—*Journal of Commerce.*

We'd still go along with Pratt & Whitney, or Rolls.

The Aborigines, the original inhabitants of Australia, now number only about 50,000. They are the descendants of the dark Stone-Age peoples found by the first explorers. In central and north Australia a few follow the nomadic ways of their ancestors and still preserve the rituals and family relationships which they have followed since time immemorial. They use the simplest of tools and their very existence in the particularly harsh surroundings they inhabit is due to an intuitive understanding and relationship with nature itself. Some have partially assimilated and work on cattle and sheep stations like the Drover *top left* while others remain completely untouched, living from Kangaroo *top right* shellfish *left* turtle eggs *far right* and honey *above.* The art of the Aborigine has not changed since Stone-Age times as the examples *right* at Bone Cave, Wessell Islands show.

NEW ZEALAND

New Zealand was discovered by Abel Tasman in 1642, and in 1769 Captain Cook visited the area and a few years later the first British settlers arrived.

The spectacular range of the Southern Alps is dominated by Mount Cook *left* which rises to over 12,000 feet. On the North Island there are three national parks. By Lake Taupo is the Tongariro National Park which includes three mildly active volcanoes, Ruapehu, Ngauruhoe *right* and Tongarior. In the middle of the North Island is a large thermal region with coloured springs, boiling mud pools and geysers. Rotorua *below* is the leading centre for both tourists and those visiting for medicinal reasons.

FIJI

Fiji comprises over 300 small islands, many uninhabited. Traditional life continues almost totally unchanged *below* such as at the Kava ceremony. All of the islands have beautiful palm beaches as at Astrolabe Bay *right* and good anchorages like the Bay of Islands *below*.

TAHITI

Tahiti is the principle island of the Society Group. Surrounded by a coral reef its scenic beauty has attracted artists and poets such as Gauguin who fled from Europe in 1891 and settled where mango, coconut and bread fruit trees grew abundantly in the rich red soil. The traditional dances *right* are still performed by the particularly beautiful Polynesian people.